Contents

How to use this book

Speech bubbles raise interesting questions that you can discuss with others in your group.

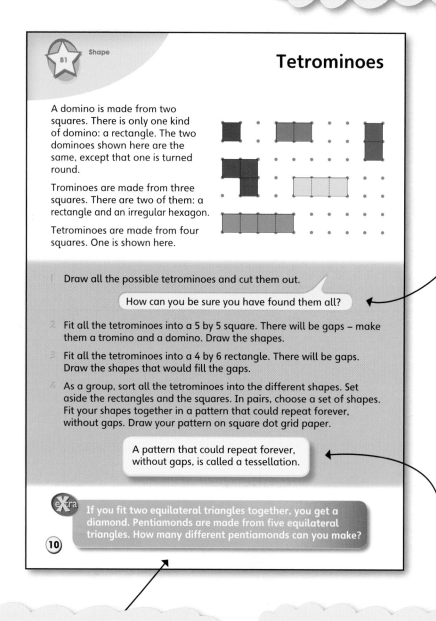

B1 Shape

Tetrominoes

A domino is made from two squares. There is only one kind of domino: a rectangle. The two dominoes shown here are the same, except that one is turned round.

Trominoes are made from three squares. There are two of them: a rectangle and an irregular hexagon.

Tetrominoes are made from four squares. One is shown here.

1 Draw all the possible tetrominoes and cut them out.

How can you be sure you have found them all?

2 Fit all the tetrominoes into a 5 by 5 square. There will be gaps – make them a tromino and a domino. Draw the shapes.

3 Fit all the tetrominoes into a 4 by 6 rectangle. There will be gaps. Draw the shapes that would fill the gaps.

4 As a group, sort all the tetrominoes into the different shapes. Set aside the rectangles and the squares. In pairs, choose a set of shapes. Fit your shapes together in a pattern that could repeat forever, without gaps. Draw your pattern on square dot grid paper.

A pattern that could repeat forever, without gaps, is called a tessellation.

eXtra If you fit two equilateral triangles together, you get a diamond. Pentiamonds are made from five equilateral triangles. How many different pentiamonds can you make?

10

If you finish the main activity before the end of the lesson, you can move on to the Extra activity.

Yellow boxes give you useful tips to help you understand the questions.

Growing on trees

Here is a tree of numbers. The larger numbers are at the base and the smallest number is at the top.

The hexagon below the tree shows the rule for changing the numbers as you move in different directions.

We have been given the rules for moves in two directions. We can use these to complete the tree.

We can then complete the hexagon to show the rules for all six directions.

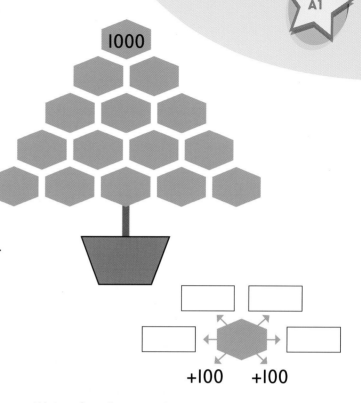

+100   +100

| Complete the first tree on PCM I. Fill in the four other rules around the hexagon.

> Does everyone's tree look the same?

2   Complete the next tree on PCM I. It has different rules!

3–4 Complete the two trees on PCM 2.
    Make up your own rules for these trees.

> What rules did other people in the group make up?

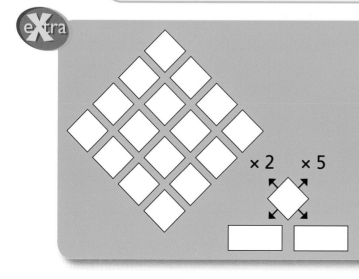

e✗tra

Copy this diamond pattern onto squared paper. Write I in the bottom box.

Complete the diamond. What do you notice about the patterns of numbers? If you start with another small number, such as 4, what patterns result?

× 2   × 5

3

Make a number

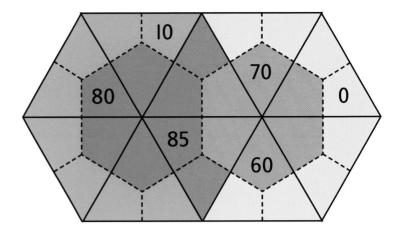

Look at this pattern.

You are going to complete the pattern. Here are the rules.

> Rule I: The three numbers in each triangle must add to 100.
> Rule 2: The numbers in the green hexagon must add to 300.
>   The numbers in the blue hexagon must add to 200.
> Rule 3: All the numbers must be multiples of 5.
> Rule 4: No repeated numbers are allowed in the same triangle.
> Rule 5: No repeated numbers are allowed in the green hexagon.
> Rule 6: No repeated numbers are allowed in the blue hexagon.

I Complete the first pattern on PCM 5, using these numbers:

0	5	5	10	10	10	15	15	20	20	25

30	35	40	45	50	50	55	55	65

2 Now look at the second pattern on the PCM. The rules are the same as before, except that the numbers in the hexagons must add to a multiple of 25. You can use any multiples of 5 to complete the pattern, but you may only use two numbers over 25. Investigate the possible totals of the numbers in your hexagons, and try to explain any patterns that you find.

3 Explore filling in the larger pattern on the PCM, using the same rules.

eXtra Return to the original problem. If the hexagon totals are not 300 and 200, many different solutions are possible. This time, find the largest possible total from adding both of the hexagon totals.

Sheets of stamps

These sheets of stamps have different values.

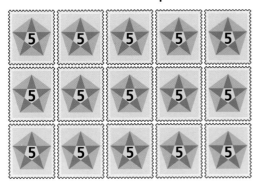

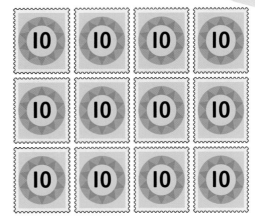

I   What is the total value of each row of 5p stamps?

2   What is the total value of the sheet of 5p stamps?

3   What is the total value of each row of 10p stamps?

4   What is the total value of the sheet of 10p stamps?

These stamps are worth 20p, 25p, 50p, £1, £2, £2·50 and £5.

Sheets can be made up of two different values of stamp.
Using any values of stamp above, work out which stamps
are used to make these totals.

5   Eight stamps with a total value of £1·20

6   Five stamps with a total value of £3·50

7   Six stamps with a total value of £20·00

Do any of these
questions have more
than one answer?

Using any values of stamp above, make the following totals using the
least number of stamps.

8   £1·90   9   £7·40   10   £19·35

**Working with a partner, create your own questions like
the ones above. Make them as hard a challenge as you
can! Pass your questions to the others in your group.**

Calculator rules

Your teacher will show you what to do if your calculator doesn't work like this.

Type the number **1** **0** into your calculator.

Press **+** **1** **0** , and then **=** .

Press **=** again.

Press **=** again.

Your calculator will keep on adding 10 every time you press **=** .

Make your calculator:

1 Go from 50 to 250 in steps of +50.

2 Go from 100 to 500 in steps of +25.

3 Go from 1000 to 800 in steps of –20.

4 Go from 5000 to 0 in steps of –500.

5 Write your own stepping patterns on strips of paper. Swap your strips with a partner, and try each other's patterns.

6 Type a 4-digit number into your calculator. Repeatedly subtract 100 until there is a 0 in the hundreds place. How would you get to a 0 in another digit place?

7 1000 schoolchildren are going on a trip. One coach company has coaches that can take 50 children. How many coaches are needed? Estimate the answer, then check it using your calculator, stepping in 50s.

8 Other companies have coaches that can take 45, 32, and 29. How many coaches are needed in each case? Estimate first.

9 Work with a partner. Can you make your calculator run through the ×5 multiplication table just by pressing = repeatedly? Try other tables, with one of you using the calculator and the other saying the multiples, for example: 7, 14, 21, …

Instead of adding or subtracting, try to work out how to make your calculator multiply again and again. Starting at 2, make it show the doubling pattern: 2, 4, 8, 16, …
What other patterns can you make in this way?

Egyptian numbers

Ancient Egyptian numbers have been found on stone walls, on pottery and on papyrus, which was a kind of paper. Egyptian numbers were made from pictures – called hieroglyphs.
Here are the hieroglyphs and our modern number equivalents.

I	10	100	1000	10 000	100 000	1 000 000

To write Egyptian numbers, the largest number is written first, but the whole number is either written:

from right to left   or   from top to bottom

46 206

4622

> What do you draw when there is a zero in the number?

Write these numbers using Egyptian hieroglyphs.

1 42   2 350   3 2401

4 13 045   5 204 000   6 1 020 030

 Use the internet to find out about the Eye of Horus and how it helped the Egyptians to represent their 'sacred fractions', starting with $\frac{1}{2}$ and $\frac{1}{4}$.

Circular counting stick

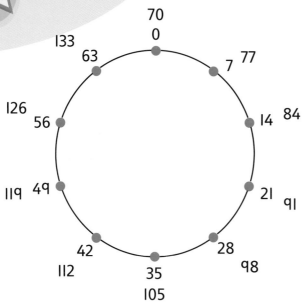

Here is a circular version of a counting stick.

When you get back to the beginning, you can just keep counting. If you are counting in 1s, you get to 10, then continue around again to 20, and so on.

The circular counting stick shown is counting in 7s, so once around gets to 70.

The pattern for the ×4 table is 4, 8, 12, 16, 20, 24, 28, 32, 36, 40.
Then you continue through 44, 48, 52, 56, 60, 64, 68, 72, 76, to 80.

1 Choose two more tables to rehearse. Continue around the circle a second time … and maybe even further. Record the patterns on PCM 6.

2 Do you notice anything about the patterns in the numbers on the first and second time around?

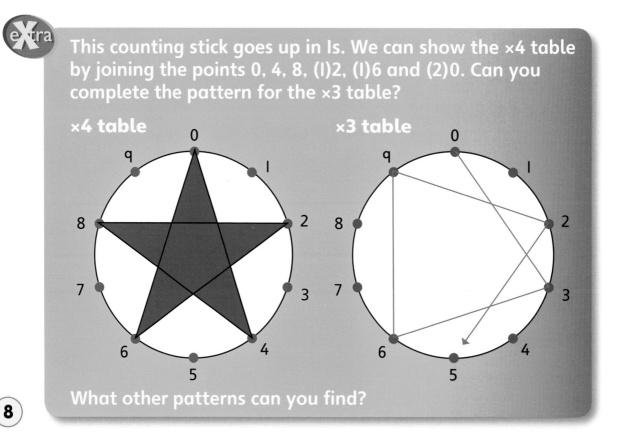

eXtra

This counting stick goes up in 1s. We can show the ×4 table by joining the points 0, 4, 8, (1)2, (1)6 and (2)0. Can you complete the pattern for the ×3 table?

×4 table

×3 table

What other patterns can you find?

Rows of houses

To make a house of numbers

- First choose two numbers, for example 6 and 4. Write them in the middle of the house.

- Add the numbers and write the sum on the roof of the house.

- Subtract the smaller number from the larger and write the difference in the bottom of the house.

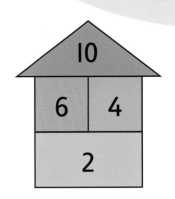

1–5 Complete the first five houses on PCM 7.

6–10 On the PCM, make up some house problems like these for others to solve. Make them as difficult as you can! Be careful to give away only two of the four numbers in each house.

To make a row of houses

- Make a house of numbers.

- Copy the numbers from the top and bottom of your house into the middle of the second house. Complete the second house.

- Use the top and bottom numbers from the second house to make the third house. Carry on this way to the end of the row.

11 Complete the row of houses on the PCM.

12 Make your own row of five houses on the PCM.

 Working in a group, make the longest row of houses you can. Take strips of houses and glue or tape them together. Use any patterns you have spotted to check your numbers. If the numbers get very large you may use a calculator to check.

Tetrominoes

A domino is made from two squares. There is only one kind of domino: a rectangle. The two dominoes shown here are the same, except that one is turned round.

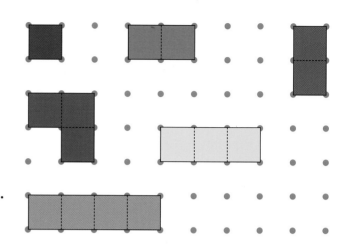

Trominoes are made from three squares. There are two of them: a rectangle and an irregular hexagon.

Tetrominoes are made from four squares. One is shown here.

1 Draw all the possible tetrominoes and cut them out.

> How can you be sure you have found them all?

2 Fit all the tetrominoes into a 5 by 5 square. There will be gaps – make them a tromino and a domino. Draw the shapes.

3 Fit all the tetrominoes into a 4 by 6 rectangle. There will be gaps. Draw the shapes that would fill the gaps.

4 As a group, sort all the tetrominoes into the different shapes. Set aside the rectangles and the squares. In pairs, choose a set of shapes. Fit your shapes together in a pattern that could repeat forever, without gaps. Draw your pattern on square dot grid paper.

> A pattern that could repeat forever, without gaps, is called a tessellation.

eXtra

If you fit two equilateral triangles together, you get a diamond. Pentiamonds are made from five equilateral triangles. How many different pentiamonds can you make?

Tile patterns

Here are four different tiles.

I Choose one of the tiles from PCM 10. Arrange the four copies
   of it to make a square. How many different patterns can you make?
   Draw your patterns so you don't forget them!

Do the four tiles on the PCM have different numbers of possible patterns?

2 What is the rule for moving along
   this frieze pattern?

A frieze is a decorative
horizontal band.

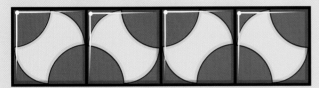

3 Use one of the four types of tile on the PCM to make your own frieze
   pattern. What rule will you use? Draw your pattern.

If you like, you could design your own pattern tile and create a frieze
pattern using it.

If you have a horizontal rule
and a vertical rule, you can
continue your pattern for
as long as you like in both
directions.
This example uses a
horizontal rule of reflection
and a vertical rule of rotation.

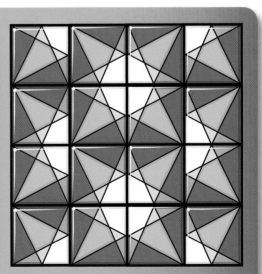

Rotation means turning.

With copies of one of the tiles,
make your own 4 by 4 pattern.

M C Escher

Maurits Cornelius Escher was an artist and mathematician. Some of his artwork uses tessellation.

Escher took simple tessellations such as one made from squares, and found ways to transform them. He took a piece from one side of the square and placed it on another side. This method is called 'put and take'.

He transformed tessellations of polygons such as squares, rhombuses, rectangles and triangles, and created more interesting tessellations.

1 Transform a square using the 'put and take' method. The resulting shape must still be able to tessellate (with no gaps)! Draw your shape and cut it out carefully.

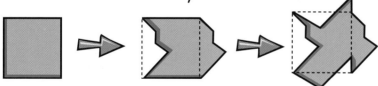

2 Use your shape to make a tessellating pattern. Once you have made your pattern, you can colour the shapes.

How do the shapes fit together?

3 Try making a tessellating pattern starting with a different polygon and using the 'put and take' method.

eXtra Use the internet to find out more about M C Escher's work with tessellations.

Body measures

1   Working with a partner, use card strips and a metre rule to measure your head circumference and your arm length.

2   Write the measurements for each member of your group in a table. Find the difference between each pair of measures.

Name	Head circumference	Arm length	Difference

3   Discuss your data.

What other pairs of body lengths could you compare?

4   Measure your height and your arm span.

5   Compare your measurements. Are they quite close in length? This often happens, though we keep changing as we grow up.

Can you think of any mammals whose measurements would be very different?

6   Measure your hand span and foot length.

7   In ancient Egypt, adult hand spans and feet were part of the measuring system. A hand span was $\frac{3}{4}$ of a foot. Look at your data. Is your hand span about $\frac{3}{4}$ of your foot length?

 eXtra

Research the ancient body measurement systems of Egypt. Collect the information that you find into a table. Include your own body measurements.

Making journeys

The map on PCM 12 shows the main towns and roads of the Isle of Wight. The diagram below it is a journey planning map, with distances in kilometres. There is a car ferry between Cowes and East Cowes.

1 Mr Shulin travels from Newport to Ryde, then to Sandown and around the coast to Yarmouth, before returning to Newport. What is the total distance of his journey?

From	To	Distance
Newport	Ryde	11 km 700 m
Newport	Shanklin	15 km 200 m
Newport	Godshill	9 km 300 m
Newport	Nilton	13 km 900 m
Newport	Freshwater	19 km 100 m
Newport	Yarmouth	16 km 100 m
Newport	Cowes	8 km 500 m
Newport	E Cowes	8 km 400 m
Ryde	Sandown	10 km 700 m
Sandown	Shanklin	3 km 500 m
Shanklin	Godshill	5 km 900 m
Shanklin	Ventnor	6 km
Ventnor	Nilton	7 km 200 m
Nilton	Freshwater	23 km 700 m
Freshwater	Yarmouth	3 km

2 This table gives a more accurate distance for each of the main roads on the island (to the nearest 100 m). What is the total distance of Mr Shulin's journey if you use this table? What is the difference between this and your answer to question 1?

3 Design another trip on the island, visiting five places. Use the map and the table to get two total distances for your trip. Compare these.

eXtra Imagine you are on a two-day holiday on the island. Decide what town to stay in. Plan trips for both days, visiting all of the places on the main road map once. You can go through Newport as often as you need, and use the Cowes to East Cowes ferry once. Record your trips and total journey distances.

Designing a survey

Tina and Amrit designed and presented a survey about cars.
They followed these five steps.

- **Decide what data to collect.** Tina and Amrit wanted to know what makes of car are owned by their classmates' families.

- **Decide how to collect the data.** They listed the different makes on a data collection sheet.

- **Collect the information.** They asked the children in their class to complete their data collection sheet.

Make	Tally
Citroen	|||| |||| ||
Fiat	||
Ford	|||| |||| ||||	
Peugeot	||
Renault	|||| ||||
Skoda	||
Vauxhall	|||

- **Decide how to present the data.** They decided to make a bar chart and a pictogram.

Makes of car owned by class 3B's families

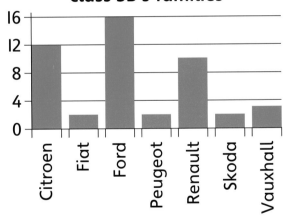

Makes of car owned by class 3B's families

Citroen	🚗 🚗 🚗
Fiat	🚗
Ford	🚗 🚗 🚗 🚗
Peugeot	🚗
Renault	🚗 🚗 🚗
Skoda	🚗
Vauxhall	🚗

Key: 🚗 = 4 cars

- **Think about the data.** Their charts showed that the most popular make of car in their survey is Ford.

> What questions can't be answered from the data?

Carry out your own survey, using the five steps above.

 Make a poster to display your survey results.

Stem-and-leaf diagrams

These were Ayesha's cricket scores for 20 innings.

21	35	9	49	24	18	27	33	16	4
38	22	26	44	21	27	30	35	24	19

This is a stem-and-leaf diagram showing the same data.

Ayesha's cricket scores

Stem	Leaves						
4	4	9					
3	0	3	5	5	8		
2	1	1	2	4	4	6	7	7
1	6	8	9				
0	4	9					

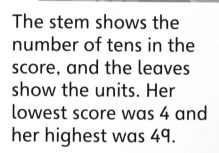

The stem shows the number of tens in the score, and the leaves show the units. Her lowest score was 4 and her highest was 49.

1. Make a stem-and-leaf diagram to show this cricketer's data.

72	95	89	94	52	81	77	88	99	57
75	60	69	82	90	92	80	57	66	91

2. Which group of scores occurs most often?

3. What is the difference between the highest and lowest scores?

4. How many more scores were in the 80s than in the 60s?

5. For each score in the 70s, how many runs was the batsman short of a century (100 runs)?

Look at this double-sided stem-and-leaf diagram. Redraw your diagram from question 1 in this way. Does it give a better picture of the data?

Leaves			Stem	Leaves		
3	2	0	1	5	8	
	4	2	0	7	7	9

Minibeasts

When biologists check the populations of different kinds of insect and other small creatures in an area, they mark out an area with lines made of string at I metre intervals. This means that the area is divided into metre-square parts.

The biologist then chooses some of these squares from different parts of the area, and uses a small vacuum device called a 'pooter' to collect all the small creatures which are in the chosen squares. Once the minibeasts in a square have been counted, they are safely returned.

On PCM I3 you will find the results of several squares in one field.

1 Make a tally chart and use it to collect the total numbers of beetles, ants, spiders and woodlice in these squares.

2 How many of each creature is there altogether?

3 Draw a bar chart or a pictogram of the data.

4 Write some questions you could ask someone else about the data.

The biologists want to know how many of each creature they should expect to find in an average metre square. To do this they look at the total number of each creature. Then they work out how many of each creature would be in one square if each of their 8 squares had the same number. How many beetles would there be? How many ants? How many woodlice? How many spiders?

Disc numbers

12   10

These two discs are numbered on both sides.
The numbers on the other sides are single digits.

$12 + 10 = 22$

By turning over one or both of the discs you can
make three other totals: 13, 17 and 18.

1 What numbers are on the back of each disc?

2 Change the numbers on the back of
the discs, but keep them single digits.
Investigate other sets of totals that
can be made.

> Do you always get
> four different totals?
> What else can happen?

These two discs have totals 12, 153, 159 and 300.

7   5

3 What are the numbers on the other sides of
these discs?

Keep one number on each disc a single digit and
find pairs of discs that make these totals.

4 10, 201, 209, 400

5 17, 347, 350, 680

> Look at the four totals that can
> be made for each pair of discs.
> Are there any patterns?

6 13, 500, 513, 1000

7 14, 481, 533, 1000

8 Make up your own pairs of numbered discs. Find their totals.
Exchange totals with others in your group and find each other's
disc numbers.

e**X**tra

Make three numbered discs so that all their totals
are different and make a consecutive pattern of
numbers, such as 9, 10, 11, 12, 13, 14, 15, 16.

Boxed number games

 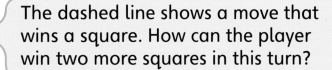

Rules

- Play in pairs.
- Each player uses a different colour.
- Take turns to join the dots vertically or horizontally.
- You win a small square when you complete it. Colour it in.
- When you win a square you have another turn straight away.
- The winner is the player with the most squares at the end.

> The dashed line shows a move that wins a square. How can the player win two more squares in this turn?

1. Play the game on a blank game board on PCM 14.

2. Play again, using the first numbered game board on PCM 14. This time, when you win a square, you win the number in that square. The player with the highest score at the end wins the game.

3. Play using the other game boards on PCM 14.

> Keep track of your scores as you play. Is there a point when you know someone has won?

> What good strategies can you find as you play these games?

 eXtra
Look at the first numbered game board on PCM 14. Look at where the biggest numbers are placed. Is there a pattern? Add each row, add each column, and add all four corners. Do you notice a key number?
Do the same for all the game boards on PCM 14. Do they all have the same property?
Use a blank grid and make up a new game board with this property. Make the key number for your game a multiple of 100.

19

Subtraction cross-number puzzles

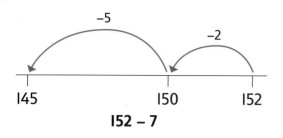

145   150   152

152 – 7

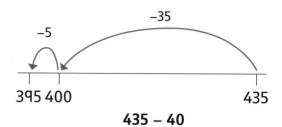

395 400   435

435 – 40

Draw number lines to find the answers to these subtractions.

1	143 – 5	2	226 – 9	3	365 – 7
4	256 – 40	5	406 – 50	6	817 – 30

7   Use these clues for the first cross-number puzzle on PCM 15.

Clues across		Clues down	
A	181 – 9	A	11 008 – 100
C	122 – 30	B	2618 – 70
E	106 – 50	D	224 – 8
F	931 – 7	G	912 – 9
G	166 – 70		
H	95 – 8		
I	512 – 80		

8   Invent similar subtraction
clues for this completed
cross-number puzzle.
Write your clues on PCM 15.

	A 1	9	B 7		C 2
D 7	7		E 8	F 1	5
G 1	0	H 4	5	0	3
I 8	6	9		J 8	7
3		K 6	7	5	

Invent your own cross-number puzzle and clues using a
blank grid on PCM 15. Keep a copy of your puzzle's solution.
Exchange puzzles with someone else in your group.

Clocks through time

Before clocks were invented, people knew roughly what part of the day it was from the position of the Sun in the sky.

The first known clocks were sundials.

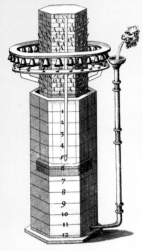

Another kind of clock was later designed, the water clock. The ancient Greeks called this 'clepsydra' meaning 'water thief'. These clocks could be used when the sun was not visible, and at night.

Mechanical clocks with cogs, gears and swinging pendulums were designed to tell the time accurately for all 24 hours of the day.

At first they had just a single pointer, like the sundial, to show the hours. People could use the pointer to work out the half and quarter hours.

Later the same approach produced a clock to show just the minutes. The pointer was longer and thinner, making it easier to read the 60-minute scale. The two clock faces were put beside each other so people could read the hour, then the minutes.

1 What time is shown on these pairs of faces?

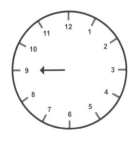 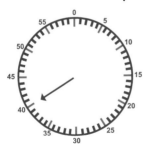  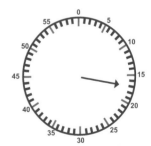

2 Research either sundials or water clocks. What are their advantages and disadvantages?

3 Design a sundial or a water clock.

Atomic clocks are now used to measure times. What can you find out about atomic clocks? Are they better than these clocks? Why?

Matching times

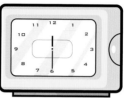

1   Start at noon, 12:00.
What time is 40 minutes earlier?
What time is 40 minutes later?

2   Start at 12:30.
What time is 50 minutes earlier?
What time is 50 minutes later?

In each of these questions the two times are the same number of minutes away from a particular time. Find that time.

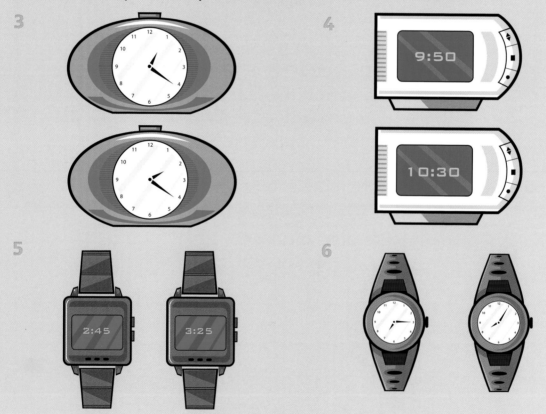

3

4   9:50   10:30

5   2:45   3:25

6

7   Complete the activity on PCM 17, matching start times, new times and numbers of minutes earlier or later.

eXtra   Make your own version of the activity on PCM 17. Use the same start times and numbers of minutes, but make up the new times. Ask a partner to complete your activity.

Linking multiplication and division

An array is a regular arrangement of rows and columns.

This arrangement of stars is called an array.

You could see this array as:

- 5 columns of 4 stars so 5 multiplied by 4, or 5 × 4

- 4 rows of 5 stars so 4 multiplied by 5, or 4 × 5

- 20 stars split into 5 columns so 20 divided by 5, or 20 ÷ 5

- 20 stars split into 4 rows so 20 divided by 4, or 20 ÷ 4

For each of these arrays, write two multiplications and two divisions.

eXtra Spread out all the cards from PCM 18. Look for pairs of cards which show families of related facts and gather the pairs together. Use blank cards from PCM 18 to complete any families which have missing facts.

Multiplication grids

Copy and complete these mini multiplication grids.

These are two-by-two grids. Work out the missing numbers.

1

×	2	3
2		
4		

2

×		
2	6	
	15	25

3

×	2	4
		8
	12	

These are three-by-three grids. Work out the missing numbers.

4

×	2	3	4
2			
3			
4			

5

×	5		
2			30
	15		
4		40	

6

×		5	8
4			
	18		48
		40	

7 Make up your own two-by-two multiplication grids. Only write four of the eight numbers. Give your puzzle to a partner to solve.

> Which four numbers can you give so that the puzzle can be solved?

8 Make puzzles using three-by-three grids. This time only give six of the 15 numbers.

eXtra

Make some puzzles using four-by-four multiplication grids. How many numbers must be revealed for the puzzles to work?

Multiplication investigation

Work out the answers to these multiplication problems.

1 [1][3] [×] [2] [=] [   ]

2 [3][4] [×] [2] [=] [   ]

> The answer to a multiplication is called the product.

3 [4][1] [×] [3] [=] [   ]

4 [1][2] [×] [4] [=] [   ]

5 Make up four more multiplication problems using the digit cards 1, 2, 3 and 4. Solve the problems and find the products.

6 Make up as many multiplication problems as you can, using just the digit cards 1, 4 and 5.

7 Investigate the possible problems that can be made from other sets of three digit cards.

> Which multiplication gives the largest product? Which gives the smallest product?

8 Choose three digit cards and use them to make three different products. Tell your partner the three products. Can they work out your three digit cards?

9 The examples below show two different ways of using the digits 2, 3 and 4 in a different arrangement. Choose three different digits and investigate the possible combinations you can make.

[2] [×] [3] [+] [4] [=] [10]

[4] [×] [2] [+] [3] [=] [11]

 eXtra With a partner, use four digit cards to create and solve harder problems, like ☐☐☐ × ☐. Use a calculator to find the products.

25

Fraction sentences

1 Place the digits 0, 1, 2 and 5 to complete this fraction sentence.

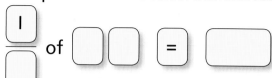

> Unit fractions are a single part of a number, like one fifth ($\frac{1}{5}$) or one sixth ($\frac{1}{6}$).

2 Work out what digits must be used to make the fraction sentence for a quarter of 12.

> A fraction of a number is the same as the fraction multiplied by the number.

3 Use digit cards to make up some more fraction sentences.

4 Write fraction sentences to work out different unit fractions of 24. Gather 24 cubes to help.

5 Choose a secret number of cubes and write at least four different unit fraction sentences with that number as the answer. See if your partner can work out what number of cubes you have.

This array shows 20p in 4 rows of 5p, or 5 columns of 4p.

The relationship between 20, 4 and 5 can be written in different ways:

Unit fraction of	Divided by	Multiplied by
$\frac{1}{4}$ of 20 = 5	20 ÷ 4 = 5	5 × 4 = 20

6 Make your own arrays. Complete the table to show the different ways of writing the relationships between the numbers in your arrays.

 e**X**tra Explore doubling all the unit fraction sentences you have written. For example, $\frac{1}{5} \times 20 = 4$, so $\frac{2}{5} \times 20 = 8$. Can you extend this idea?

Doubling and halving shapes

These two shapes are both hexagons.

Are they the same shape?

Compare their areas.

> How many small triangles are in each shape?

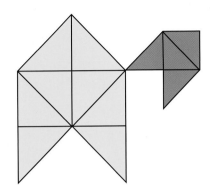

The hexagons were drawn using the grid on PCM 20.
Use the grid to investigate doubling and halving shape areas.

1 Draw a shape on the grid. Then draw the same shape but half of the size.

2 Double the shape. Now try doubling again, and again, to produce shapes with 4 times and 8 times the area.

3 Try doubling and halving other shapes.

> Look for a pattern.
> Apart from getting larger or smaller, what else does enlarging on the grid do to all of the shapes?

These two arrowhead quadrilaterals were drawn on the other grid on PCM 20. The area of the larger one is 3 times the area of the smaller one.

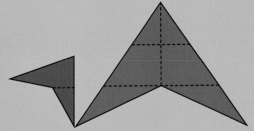

Use the grid and investigate finding other enlargements where two shapes are the same, but one is 3 times bigger than the other.

Rounding

1   These headlines all describe the crowd at a local football match. The attendance was 7374 exactly, but the number has been rounded differently in each case.

Work out which headline has rounded the crowd to the nearest 10, 100, 500 and 1000.

> **Capacity crowd 7500 fill stadium**
>
> **7370 attend local final**
>
> **Crowd of 7400 is biggest ever**
>
> **7000 SEE UNITED WIN**

2   Round 5485 to the nearest 10, 100, 500 and 1000.

3   There are 2374 cucumbers. How many crates can be filled with 100 cucumbers in each?

4   How many £10 notes are needed to pay a bill of £134·67?

5   There are 972 soldiers to be carried. How many trucks are needed if each truck can carry 50 soldiers?

These numbers have been rounded to the nearest 50.
What is the highest and lowest exact number they could be?

6   250   7   800   8   4750

These measures have been rounded down to the nearest 10 cm.
What is the longest exact length they could be?

9   70 cm   10   1 metre   11   550 cm

These amounts of money have been rounded up to the nearest £10.
What is the lowest exact amount they could be?

12   £200   13   £820   14   £450

eXtra   Think of some examples where numbers, money, or measures may need to be rounded. Do the numbers need to be rounded up or down? How exact do the rounded numbers need to be?

Ordering numbers

Which amount in each set is the smallest?
Which is the largest? Write them in order,
from smallest to largest.

| 1 | 2198 | 3167 | 3204 | 2222 | 3189 |

| 2 | £11·45 | £10·96 | £10·49 | £11·12 | £11·01 |

Write a number between each pair of numbers.

3 45 210 and 45 219

4 13 489 and 14 503

5 67 675 and 76 682

6 10 705 and 11 698

Find the number exactly half-way between each pair of numbers.

7  255 and 263

8  388 and 400

9  1425 and 1441

10  5702 and 6696

Can you come up with a rule for
finding the half-way number?

Work with a partner to design a set of six cards that make
a loop. Use all of the ideas from the set of cards from
PCM 21, but use amounts of money. Which is the smallest
amount? Which is the largest? Find the amount exactly
half-way between. Swap sets with another pair.

Timelines

Timelines are periods of time set out on a scale. They are used to show when important events occurred over a period of time.

2000	2001	2002	2003	2004	2005	2006	2007	2008	2009	2010

1 Draw a timeline of the important events in your lifetime.

2 Make a timeline of the last 100 years.
- Join paper strips to make a strip more than 1 metre long.
- Draw a 1 metre line along the paper strips, and mark every 10 cm.
- Mark the ends 1910 and 2010. Write the decades (1920, 1930, ...) on the 10 cm markers.

3 Mark some of these historic events of the past 100 years on your timeline. Use reference books and the internet to find some more events and dates to add to your timeline.

1914	Start of First World War
1926	Women over 21 get the vote in Britain
1939	Start of Second World War
1953	First successful ascent of Mount Everest
1966	England wins Football World Cup
1969	Man first walks on the Moon
1989	Fall of the Berlin Wall
2000	World population tops 6 billion people
2008	Britain wins 19 gold medals at Beijing Olympics

eXtra

We use the Gregorian calendar, but there are four other main calendars used around the world. Work out when the events in your 100-year timeline occurred according to these other calendars. Use this information to help you.

Calendar	Gregorian	Chinese	Hebrew	Indian	Islamic
Year	2010	4708	5770	5111	1430

Counting sequences

With a partner, try these counting challenges.

Take turns to write out the sequence. Your partner puts the counting rule into a calculator and checks your sequence against the calculator display.

1 Start at 100, count on in 10s to 200.   Repeat +10

2 Start at 200, count on in 5s to 250.   Repeat +5

3 Start at 500, count back in 50s to 0.   Repeat −50

4 Start at 1000, count back in 100s to 0.   Repeat −100

5 Start at 45, count on in 500s to 5045.   Repeat +500

6 Start at 9075, count back in 1000s to 75.   Repeat −1000

Choose whether to count in steps of 5, 10, 50, 100, 500 or 1000, to get from one number in each pair to the other.

Which step size did you choose? Do you need to count on or back?

7 0 and 350

8 0 and 140

9 250 and 1250

10 800 and 8800

11 Choose two of your sequences. Record the numbers in the sequence and write the number of steps needed.

eXtra

Choose a start number and a step size. Count on 10 steps and find the end number. Tell your partner the start and end numbers. Can they work out the size of step needed to get from the start to the end in 10 steps? Swap roles.

31

Olympic rings

The Olympic flag has a white background, with five intersecting rings of blue, yellow, black, green and red. This design symbolises the five inhabited continents of the world.

1 Add the numbers in each ring. What do you find?

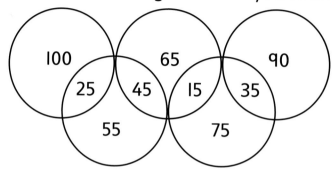

Write these numbers in the rings on PCM 23 so that the rings in each set have the same total.

2 1, 2, 3, 4, 5, 6, 7, 8 and 9

3 2, 3, 4, 5, 6, 7, 8, 10 and 11

What patterns can you see?

4 15, 21, 27, 33, 39, 45, 51, 66 and 72

5 Which number is missing from this set?

21, 29, 37, 45, 53, 61, 69 and 98

6 Which number is not needed in this set?

20, 30, 40, 50, 60, 70, 80, 90, 100 and 110

7 Find other sets of nine numbers that give equal totals when placed in the five rings. Try totals such as 250 or 1000.

eXtra Use the last set of rings on PCM 23 to explore possible sets of numbers to make equal totals in a loop of six rings.

Using multiples to add and subtract

Complete these calculations.

1	50 + 35	2	75 – 30	3	45 + 25
4	100 – 55	5	65 + 30	6	85 – 65

7 Make up some additions and subtractions of your own.

You can use 90 – 35 to work out 91 – 33.

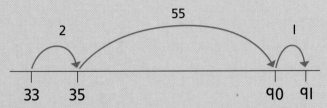

$$91 – 33 = 55 + 2 + 1 = 58$$

Use this method and your answers to questions 1–6 to complete these calculations.

8	52 + 36	9	77 – 28	10	43 + 26
11	99 – 53	12	67 + 29	13	87 – 64

Now work out these subtractions. Remember that every whole number is 1 or 2 away from a multiple of 5 or 10. How much do you need to adjust each question by to find the answer?

14	67 – 39	15	82 – 46	16	94 – 28

17 Use your own examples to investigate this. Try some examples with amounts of money.

How long ago did these historical events take place? Work out how many years before 2000 each date is, then adjust the answer to get to the year we are in now.

1914   Start of First World War
1953   First successful ascent of Mount Everest
1966   England wins Football World Cup
1989   Fall of the Berlin Wall

Adding and subtracting

Solve these calculations.

1 1300 + ☐ = 2000   2 810 + ☐ = 900

3 260 + ☐ = 600   4 470 + ☐ = 1200

> A decade number is a multiple of 10.
> 140 and 60 are two decade numbers that total 200.

5 Find all the possible pairs of decade numbers that total 200.

You can pay for each item with a £1 coin, a £5 note or a £10 note. Decide which to use for each item and then work out how much change you will get. Add your change to the money already in the purse. For each item, how much money do you have left in total?

6 £3·99   £3·21

7 45p   £5·05

8 FAIRY TALES £7·25   34p

9 £6·50   £11·20

10 66p   £5·55 0

11 £2·20   25p

12 Choose a multiple of 5 between 5 and 100. How many subtractions can you make with this answer?

> What rule could you use to help you to make subtractions with the same answer?

eXtra

Use five digit cards to make additions and subtractions involving a 3-digit and a 2-digit number. For example, you can use 2, 3, 5, 6 and 8 to make 265 + 38 = ☐, ☐ − 65 = 218 and ☐ − ☐ = 205. Make as many additions and subtractions as you can using five digits, and fill in the missing numbers. Repeat with five different numbers.

34

Making 3D stars

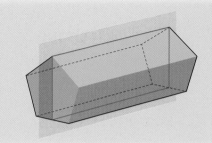

1 Does this regular hexagon have any more lines of symmetry?

2 What is the rule for lines of symmetry of regular polygons with an even number of sides? An odd number of sides?

3 This is one plane of symmetry of a pentagonal prism. How many does it have in total?

4 Is there a link between the number of planes of symmetry of a prism and the number of lines of symmetry of its polygon?

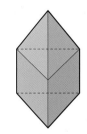

This is a triangular prism. A pyramid made of isosceles triangles has been added to one end of the prism. If you add a pyramid to each face of the prism, you will get a star-shaped polyhedron.

> A polyhedron is a 3D shape with flat faces and straight edges.

This table shows how the number of vertices and faces changes as each pyramid cap is added.

	Vertices	Faces
Start with a triangular prism:	6	5
Add a triangular-based pyramid:	7	7
Add a triangular-based pyramid:	8	9
Add a square-based pyramid:	9	12
Add a square-based pyramid:	10	15
Add a square-based pyramid:	11	18

5 Make a similar table for a regular hexagonal prism.

6 Look for patterns in the tables. Use them to work out how many vertices the star polyhedron made from a regular pentagonal prism would have. How many faces would it have?

As a group, explore the planes of symmetry of a cube. Start by thinking about the lines of symmetry of a square.

35

The Soma cube

In 1936, a Danish poet and scientist called Piet Hein invented the Soma cube. The Soma cube is a 3 by 3 by 3 cube made from seven shapes. The seven shapes are all made from three or four smaller cubes. None of the seven shapes are cuboids.

1 Can you make the seven shapes? Remember that each shape must be made from three or four cubes, and none of them must be a cuboid.

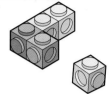

Join whole faces, don't twist the cubes.

2 Try to use your shapes to make a Soma cube.

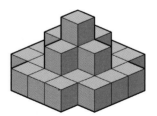

Your shapes can also be used to make other 3D shapes.

3 Make a symmetrical 3D shape using all of your shapes.

4 Make these 3D shapes using all of your shapes.

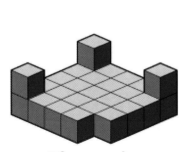

The castle

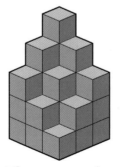

The crystal

The pyramid

eXtra

Draw a hexagon on triangle dot paper. Join three vertices to the central dot, so that it looks like a cube. Shapes made from cubes can be drawn on dot paper like this. Draw some of your shapes on the dot paper.

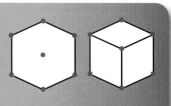

Prisms and anti-prisms

Here are the nets of a cuboid and a triangular prism.

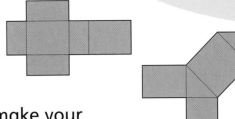

> A net is folded to make a 3D shape.

Copy these nets onto squared paper and make your own cuboid and triangular prism.

Look at the nets on PCM 25.

1 Imagine what each net would look like folded. Would it make a complete polyhedron? If not, change the diagram so that it will.

2 Cut out the nets and make the polyhedra. What are they called?

Some polyhedra are prisms and some are anti-prisms.

The diagram shows a pentagonal prism and a pentagonal anti-prism. Compare them and answer these questions.

A pentagonal prism   **A pentagonal anti-prism**

3 How are they the same? How are they different?

4 What do you notice about the numbers of vertices of each?

5 Do they share any planes of symmetry?

6 Compare some other prisms and anti-prisms, and complete the tables on PCM 25. Add some shapes of your own.

7 Are there patterns in the number of vertices, edges and faces?

> Starting with a pentagonal anti-prism, build on two pentagonal pyramids with equilateral triangle faces, so that the pentagons are hidden. What 3D polyhedron have you made?

Calibrating capacities

Your task is to change a plain plastic bottle into a measuring bottle. This is called calibrating.

You need: strips of sticky paper, lentils, a 2 litre bottle, a 100 ml bottle and a 50 ml bottle.

- Stick a strip of paper vertically to the side of your 2 litre bottle.

- Fill the 100 ml bottle with lentils. Pour them into the 2 litre bottle. Make sure the lentils are level. Mark 100 ml on the strip of paper, by the top of the pile of lentils.

> To make it easier to pour the lentils, cut the tip off a cone of paper to make a funnel.

- Complete your scale by marking 100 ml intervals until your bottle is full of lentils.

> Does everyone need the same amount of lentils to make a litre?

You now have a scale that will measure to the nearest 100 ml. Can you use the 50 ml bottle to improve on this?

Use your bottle to find the capacities of some other containers.

> You may need to estimate between two intervals.

> Can you measure out 25 ml of lentils using the 50 ml and 100 ml bottles? What about 10 ml?

e**X**tra

Make a triangle like this one from card and squared paper. How can you use it to measure the inside width of circular bottles, screw-top jars and containers?

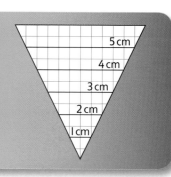

5 cm
4 cm
3 cm
2 cm
1 cm

Calculating capacities

1   What is one and a half litres in millilitres?

2   What is one and a quarter litres in millilitres?

3   What is 2000 millilitres in litres?

4   What is 750 millilitres as a fraction of a litre?

> How did you work out your answers to questions 1–4?

True or false?

5   A $\frac{1}{4}$ litre bottle of medicine will fill fifty 5 ml spoonfuls.

6   A 2·5 litre bottle contains the same as nine 300 ml bottles.

7   Six bottles containing 250 ml will fill a 1·5 litre container.

8   Find two pairs of containers that have the same capacity.

9   List the containers from smallest to largest capacity.

10 Work out the differences between the capacities of containers next to each other in your list.

For example: *The 250 ml bottle is next to the 300 ml. The difference between them is 50 ml.*

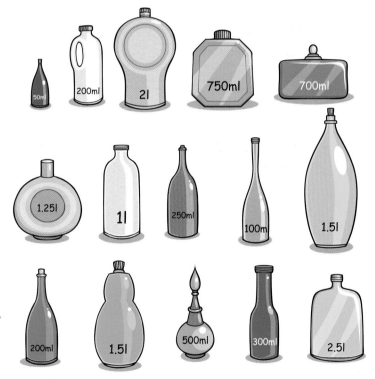

 How many 100 ml bottles can be filled from containers with these capacities?

    1 litre   1·5 litres   2 litres   5 litres   10 litres

How many 150 ml bottles can be filled?
Make up some more questions like this.

Record times

Look at PCM 26. It shows the results of some sports events.

Look at the records for the modern triathlon.

1 To the nearest half-minute, how many minutes did each record triathlon take?

2 Use your answer to question I to work out roughly how different these records are.

3 Work out the exact difference in minutes and seconds.

4–6 Answer the same questions for the marathon.

Look at the records for the 100 metre sprint.

7 To the nearest tenth of a second, how many seconds did each record sprint take?

8 Use your answer to question I to work out roughly how different these records are.

9 Work out the exact difference using a calculator.

10–12 Answer the same questions for the 400 metre sprint.

13 How much slower was the fastest lap in the 2008 British Grand Prix than the fastest lap in 2009?

14 How many days did the Round the World Clipper race take in 2007–08?

 In 2008 Portsmouth FC started playing in the FA Cup, in Round 3 when there were 64 clubs in the competition. They won the cup. They did not draw any matches. Each team played one match in each round. Each match lasted for 90 minutes. How many matches did they play? How many hours and minutes did they play altogether?

Box-and-whisker plots

PCM 28 shows the results of a 10 000 m race.

I Find the fastest time and the slowest time. What is the difference between them?

> The difference between the fastest and slowest time is called the **range**.

A box-and-whisker plot can be used to show the athletes' times.

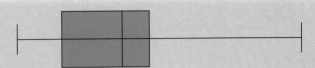

2 On the squared paper on PCM 28, draw a scale from 29 min 50 s to 32 min 30 s, marked off in 10 second intervals.

> This scale should be 16 squares long.

3 Mark two vertical 'whiskers' to show the fastest and slowest times. Join them with a horizontal line.

4 Find who finished in the middle. Mark her time with a vertical line.

> The middle value is called the **median**.

5 The field is now divided into two halves. Find who finished in the middle of each half. Mark their times with two vertical lines and join them to make a box.

> The middle values in the two halves are called the **quartiles**.

> This is called the **interquartile range**.

6 Find the difference between the two quartiles.

 Here is a box-and-whisker plot for another group of athletes. Use it to find:
- the winner's time
- the range
- the median time
- the quartile times
- the interquartile range.

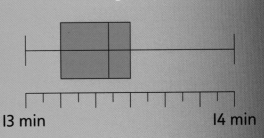

13 min   14 min

Star names and real names

Bob Dylan

Bob Dylan's real name was Robert Zimmerman.

Tina Turner

Tina Turner is really called Anna Mae Bullock.

Look at the list of star names and real names on PCM 29.

1 Find the number of letters in each name.

2 Make two frequency tables, one to show the lengths of the star names and the other to show the lengths of the real names.

3 Make two bar charts from your frequency tables.

Use your frequency tables and bar charts to answer these questions.

4 Are the star names longer or shorter than the real names?

Why do you think this is?

5 What is the most common length of star name?

6 What is the most common length of real name?

7 What is the shortest length of star name? And the longest?

8 What is the shortest length of real name? And the longest?

eXtra Tom Cruise's star name is five letters shorter than his real name. Explore the difference in length for each pair of names.

Higher number squares

You can use the 701–800 square on PCM 30 to add multiples of 10.

Start with your finger on 723.   **723**
Move downwards three spaces.   **753**
You have just traced out: **723 + 30 = 753**

How would you trace out 751 + 40?

How would you trace out a subtraction?

Use the 701–800 square to help you do these calculations.

1   719 + 41   First work out 719 + 40.

2   738 + 49   3   762 + 31   4   753 + 39
5   792 – 41   6   784 – 51   7   758 – 39

8   Use digit cards, starting with 7, to make some similar additions and subtractions. Solve them and show how you did it.

| 7 | | | + | | | or | 7 | | | – | | |

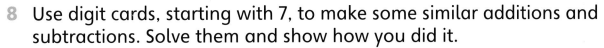

Use the 1201–1300 square on PCM 30 to do these calculations.

9   1234 + 61   First work out 1234 + 60.

10   1294 – 49   11   1244 + 48   12   1277 – 58

13   Use digit cards to make and solve some similar problems.

| 1 | 2 | | | + | | | or | 1 | 2 | | | – | | |

 e**X**tra

Explore ways of using the money grid on PCM 30 to add or subtract £100 or £200, and amounts near £100 and £200 (such as £99, £101·75, £205, £199·95).

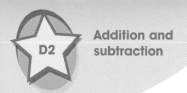

Squares to zero

This square has four numbers at its corners, and the mid-points of each side are marked.

> The mid-points are at the middle of each side.

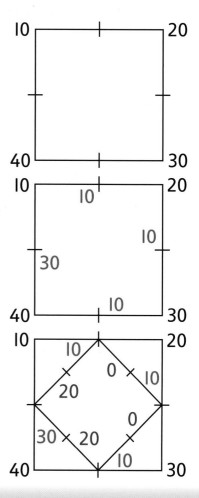

1 PCM 31 shows a copy of the square.
   Find the differences between the numbers in the corners and write them at the mid-points.

2 Join the mid-points to make a new square inside the first square.
   Find the differences for this square and write them at the mid-points.

3 Continue until all the numbers are 0.
   How many squares have you drawn altogether?

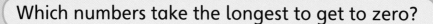

4 Write four numbers between 0 and 50 in the corners of the blank square on PCM 31. How many squares do you draw to get to 0?

> Who has the most squares?

> Which numbers take the longest to get to zero?

5 Work together to investigate what starting numbers will result in the maximum number of squares.

> Only use starting numbers between 0 and 50.

 Investigate whether you can get to zero with other regular shapes, for example equilateral triangles, regular pentagons and regular hexagons.

Addition walls

This addition number wall starts with 15, 25 and 35.

It is partly completed.

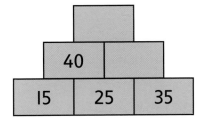

Can you see the rule for completing the wall?

1   Complete the wall on PCM 32.

2   Make another wall with the same top number as the wall in question 1.

3   Compare your wall with others. Are there any patterns?

4–5 Complete the two three-brick-base walls on the PCM.

6–7 Complete the two four-brick-base walls on the PCM.

8   Make a three-brick-base wall as a puzzle for your partner. Only fill in three numbers. Where can the three numbers be placed?

9   Make a four-brick-base wall for your partner to solve. How many numbers must you give? Where can they be placed?

10 A four-brick-base wall has the numbers 9, 25, 49 and 81 in the bottom row. Explore what happens depending on the order of these four numbers. What are the possible top numbers? Do any orders have the same top number?

A three-brick-base wall has the top number 100. The centre number on the base is 30. What numbers can the other bricks be? Find as many possible walls as you can. Is there a pattern?

45

Magic numbers

Mathematicians have long explored magic numbers. The first magic squares were found in China thousands of years ago. 'Magic' means that the numbers are arranged so that each line of numbers has the same total – the magic number.

1 This five-pointed star can be filled in with numbers from 1 to 12. Every number is different. Complete the star on PCM 34 so that all five lines of numbers have the same total.

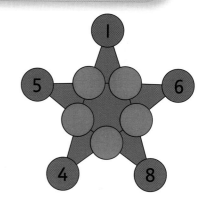

2 Which two numbers less than 12 are not used? What is the magic number?

3 The second star on PCM 34 has the numbers 6, 8, 9, 10 and 12 on its outer points. Complete the magic star using the numbers 1, 2, 3, 4 and 5. What is the magic number?

4 Use these numbers to make a five-pointed star with the magic number 28 on PCM 34.

1 3 4 5 7 8 9 10 11 12

There are 12 different stars that you can make.

Compare your star with others. Are they all different?

5 Use these numbers to complete the six-pointed star with the magic number 26 on PCM 34.

1 2 3 4 5 6 7 8 9 10 11 12

There are 30 stars that you can make. Try putting 4, 1, 3 and 2 in the outer points.

extra Write the numbers 1–10 anywhere in a blank five-pointed star. Work out the total for each line of numbers. Tell your partner the totals and see if they can make your star. If they need a clue, tell them where one or two numbers go.

Digital roots

1   Write four 3-digit numbers in the first row of the first table on PCM 35.

2   Add 99 to each number. What happens to the digits?

3   Now subtract 99 from each number. What happens to the digits?

> Is there a simple way to add or subtract 99? What about 98?

4   In the first row of the second table on PCM 35, write the digital root of each of the 3-digit numbers you wrote for question 1.

5   Now write the digital root of each of your answers to questions 2 and 3. What do you notice?

6   Find the digital root if you add or subtract 98 from each of your 3-digit numbers instead. What do you notice?

> The digital root of a number is the single-digit number that you get by adding its digits.
>
> For example, the digital root of 621 is 9.

> What happens to the digital root of a number if you keep adding 99 to that number? What about 98?

7   Write some 4-digit numbers. What happens to the digital root when you add or subtract these numbers?

     99   909   990   999

eXtra Write two 4-digit numbers. Write their digital roots. Keep trying different 4-digit numbers until you find two that both have digital roots of 9. Add the two numbers and find the digital root of the total. What do you notice?

Ants and elephants

Ants are between 1 mm and 5 mm long. There are about 2 billion ants on Earth.

African elephants are between 3 m and 4 m high. There are about 660 000 African elephants on Earth.

Living things come in many different shapes and sizes. Use the information on PCM 37 to complete the chart, following these steps.

1 Find an animal that is about 10 times the size of an ant.

2 Find some animals that are about 10 times bigger than that.

3 Repeat for 10 times bigger until you reach the end.

> When do you reach the size of an elephant?

4 Which living things are 10 times smaller than an ant?

5 Which living things are 10 times smaller than that?

6 Repeat for 10 times smaller until you reach the end.

Look at your table. Which living things are:

7 100 times larger than an ant?

8 1000 times larger than an ant?

9 100 times smaller than an elephant?

10 1000 times smaller than an elephant?

11 Can you find two living things where one is a million times larger than the other?

e**X**tra Use books or the internet to find things on Earth and in Space that are 10 times bigger than the largest living thing on your chart. Then find things that are 10 times smaller than the smallest.

Missing-number multiplications and divisions

These multiplications are each made using three different digit cards.
What are the missing digits?

1 ☐ ☐ × 5 = 65

2 ☐ ☐ × 4 = 92

3 ☐ ☐ × ☐ = 36

4 Use another three different digits and explore using your digit cards in these places. Find the products.

☐ ☐ × ☐ = ☐

> How many different multiplications can you make?

Tell a partner the products. Can they say which digits you used?

These divisions are each made using three different digit cards.
What are the missing digits?

5 ☐ ☐ ÷ 9 = 5

6 ☐ ☐ ÷ 2 = 17

7 ☐ ☐ ÷ 5 = 7

Complete these calculations. What patterns can you see? Why?

8 ☐ ☐ × 2 = 32

9 3 2 ÷ 2 = ☐

10 ☐ ☐ × 6 = 66

11 6 6 ÷ 6 = ☐

 eXtra

Explore further problems, using digit cards and combining multiplications and divisions. For example, use one set of digit cards to complete this calculation in as many ways as you can:

☐ ☐ ÷ ☐ × ☐ = ☐

Multiples of 3, 6 and 9

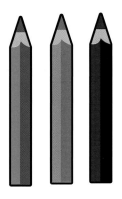

1 Use the 1–100 square on PCM 3 as follows:
   - draw a blue stripe on multiples of 3
   - draw a black stripe on multiples of 6
   - draw a red stripe on multiples of 9.

2 Which numbers only have a blue stripe?

3 Which numbers have blue and black stripes, but not red?

4 Which numbers have blue and red stripes, but not black?

5 Which numbers have blue, red and black stripes?

> Can any number be coloured black or red but not blue?

Look at the right-hand column of the 1–100 square. These are called the decade numbers.

6 What decade numbers are multiples of 3? What colours are they?

7 Find the numbers that are 3 more than each of these decade numbers. What colours are these?

8 Find the numbers that are 3 less than each of these decade numbers. What colours are these?

> Is there a pattern?

eXtra What happens with multiples of 3, 6 and 9 on other number squares? Try the 701–800 and 1201–1300 number squares on PCM 30 and any other squares that you have. Which squares have the same pattern as the 1–100 square? Which have a similar pattern to the 1–100 square? How are they different?

Escape from 100

Use this rule: ? ⟶ × 3, + 1 ⟶ ?

What are the output numbers when the input numbers are:

1 4   2 9   3 10

What are the input numbers when the output numbers are:

4 34   5 37   6 100

7 This flowchart uses the rule × 3, + 1.

Use the Rule A flowchart on PCM 38 to find out which numbers in a 1–100 square are trapped and which can escape. Can you find a pattern?

Join the trapped numbers with arrows to make a chain of numbers.

8 Repeat for the Rule B flowchart on PCM 39.

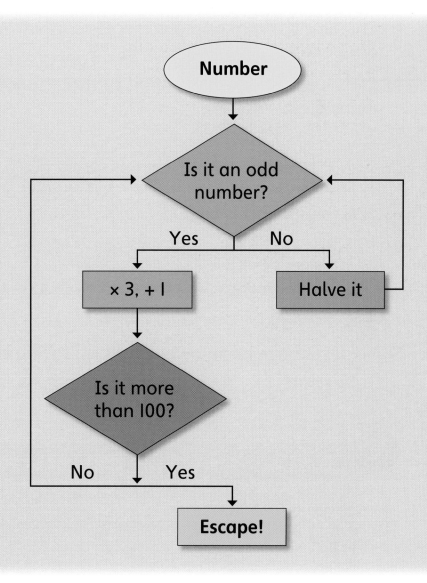

Make your own flowchart like these to explore a different rule.

Fractions of quantities

Nihal eats three pieces from each of these chocolate bars.
What fraction of each bar does Nihal eat?

1  2  3

4 Charlie eats twice as many pieces as Nihal. What fraction of each bar does Charlie eat?

5 Make up some other fractions of these chocolate bars and say how many pieces they are.

Copy and complete these fractions. Work out each part separately. Write < or > in the box to show which part is bigger.

> means is more than

< means is less than

6 $\frac{1}{2}$ of 26 ☐ $\frac{1}{4}$ of 48

7 $\frac{1}{3}$ of 27 ☐ $\frac{1}{2}$ of 20

8 $\frac{3}{4}$ of 24 ☐ $\frac{1}{2}$ of 32

9 $\frac{2}{6}$ of 42 ☐ $\frac{1}{4}$ of 44

Some prices have been lowered. Which saving is bigger?

10 $\frac{1}{3}$ off £6·99 or $\frac{2}{5}$ off £5·80

11 $\frac{1}{10}$ off £87·50 or $\frac{1}{3}$ off £26·40

 Work out some of these fractions of £60. Write out your fractions in order of size, and record them as a chain of fractions with < or = between each pair.

$\frac{1}{2}$ $\frac{1}{3}$ $\frac{2}{3}$ $\frac{1}{4}$ $\frac{2}{4}$ $\frac{3}{4}$ $\frac{1}{5}$ $\frac{2}{5}$ $\frac{3}{5}$ $\frac{4}{5}$ $\frac{1}{6}$ $\frac{2}{6}$ $\frac{3}{6}$ $\frac{4}{6}$ $\frac{5}{6}$

$\frac{1}{10}$ $\frac{2}{10}$ $\frac{3}{10}$ $\frac{4}{10}$ $\frac{5}{10}$ $\frac{6}{10}$ $\frac{7}{10}$ $\frac{8}{10}$ $\frac{9}{10}$

Fractions

Rounding and estimating

34 + 58   round to the nearest 10   30 + 60 = 90

Estimate the answers, using the rounding method shown.

1   46 + 87   2   64 + 93   3   81 + 47

Estimate the answers, first rounding the amounts to the nearest pound, then to the nearest 10p.

4   £4·46 + £1·33   5   £8·29 + £2·77   6   £6·66 + £3·27

419	326	457	286
694	126	438	164

73	47	61	43
82	58	71	38

7   Choose a number from each cloud. Round each to the nearest 10.
Add the rounded numbers. Repeat using different pairs.

8   Repeat, but this time find the difference between the pairs.

£3·23
£1·88   £8·12
£4·87   £9·29
£5·76   £3·75
£5·21

62p
37p   74p
49p   95p
28p   53p
86p

9   Choose an amount from each star. Round each to the nearest 10p.
Add the rounded amounts. Repeat using different pairs.

10   Repeat, but this time find the difference between the amounts.

11   Play the estimating game on PCM 41.

eXtra

Play the estimating game on PCM 41. If the answer is not between your two estimates, you get 0 points. Out of the players whose estimates are right, the one whose two estimates are closest together gets 10 points. If two or more players 'tie' they get 5 points each.

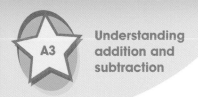
Take three numbers

Choose two of these numbers:

347   581   465

- Add them to find their sum.

- Subtract to find their difference.

- Add the sum and the difference.

What do you notice?

- Repeat the first three steps for all the possible pairs you can make using the three numbers.

- From the three subtractions, you now have three new numbers. Repeat the first three steps with these numbers.

460   890   730   240   650   380

1 Investigate the sums and differences of numbers.
   Choose three numbers from the green group above. Call this set A.

- Step 1   Make three pairs of numbers from set A.

- Step 2   Add each pair. Keep the totals. Call this set B.

- Step 3   Find the differences between each pair.
           Keep these three differences and call this set C.

You now have six new numbers: three from the additions (set B) and three from the differences (set C).

2 Take sets B and C through the three steps of the process to make new sets of numbers.

Is there a pattern?

3 Choose another three 3-digit multiple of 10 and repeat question 1.

e**X**tra   The activity started with three numbers which led to six numbers, and then 12 numbers. Explore what happens if it starts with other numbers. What happens with two, four or five starting numbers? What do you notice?

Fibonacci's pattern

Leonardo of Pisa (1170–1250) was a mathematician who was born in Italy and educated in North Africa. He was better known by his nickname, Fibonacci.

Fibonacci played an important role in reviving ancient mathematics, and came up with lots of new ideas of his own.

Fibonacci is famous for discovering this pattern of numbers: 1, 1, 2, 3, 5, 8, …

1   Explore how the numbers in Fibonacci's pattern grow.
    Can you explain how it works?

2   Continue the pattern up to at least 100.

3   Using the same rule, try pairs of starting numbers other than 1 and 1.
    Work out the first eight numbers in your pattern. Compare your
    Fibonacci-type pattern with others in your group.

Complete these Fibonacci-type patterns.

4   5, 6, ?, ?   5   2, ?, 12, ?   6   ?, 11, ?, 30

7   1, ?, ?, 21   8   ?, 15, ?, 37, ?   9   7, ?, ?, 39, ?

10 8, ?, ?, ?, 100

Explore the properties of the numbers of the original Fibonacci pattern. Look at where the multiples of 2, 3 and 4 occur. Describe any patterns you find and use these to make a prediction about where the multiples of 5 will occur. Check your prediction.

Think of a number

This TOAN machine doubles any number that goes into it.

> TOAN is short for Think Of A Number.

What are the outputs when these numbers go in?

1 9   2 26   3 35

What numbers were put in if these are the outputs?

4 14   5 26   6 42

The first part of this TOAN machine doubles numbers and the second part of it adds 1.

These numbers have either gone into the TOAN machine or they have come out.

50	49	75	289
193	37	101	24

7 Find pairs that go together as input and output numbers. Two numbers will be left over – work out their matching input or output numbers. Copy and complete the table.

Input	Output

8 Make your own TOAN machine, which adds or subtracts a number, and combine it with a doubling machine. Input five different numbers and find their outputs. Make a set of eight numbers as above. Swap your TOAN machines and set of eight numbers with someone else in your group. Solve each other's set.

 eXtra

Create more complicated TOANs that link more than two machines. You could have two doubling machines and one adding or subtracting machine, or one doubling machine and two adding or subtracting machines. You can put them in any order.

Four square

1   Choose two dots on dotted paper, not on the same line of dots.

2   Join the dots with a straight line. This is the first side of a square. The dots are the vertices (corners).

3   Where could the next sides go? Find the dots at their corners and join them to make the sides.

4   Draw a line to join the ends and complete the square.

> Can you make a different square using the same first line?

5   Explore some other lines as starting points for squares of different sizes.

The four triangles around the edge of your square are all the same. They can be joined in pairs into rectangles whose areas can easily be found. By subtracting these from the area of the surrounding square, you find the area of the blue square. In this example, each of the triangles has an area of 1·5 squares.

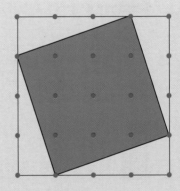

6   Use this method to find the area of some of your squares.

7   If you have not already drawn a square of area 13 squares, try to find the line that makes it.

8   Make squares with areas of 17, 20 and 25 squares.

Draw a line to join two dots, at an angle. Draw an identical line further down the paper. The first line is the diagonal of a square, not one of its sides. Draw the square and find its area. The second line is the side of a square. Draw the other sides and work out the area of this square. Compare the two areas. Explore the areas of other pairs of squares, where the same line is used as a diagonal in one square and a side in the other. Is there a pattern?

Multiplication and division cross-number puzzles

1 Use these clues to solve this cross-number puzzle.
   Write your answers on the first grid on PCM 43.

Clues across	Clues down
A 42 × 4	**A** 130 × 8
D 160 ÷ 8	**B** 328 ÷ 4
E 29 × 8	**C** 160 × 8
G 256 ÷ 4	**D** 653 × 4
H 144 ÷ 8	**F** 395 × 8
I 26 × 4	**J** 384 ÷ 8
K 240 ÷ 4	
L 105 × 8	

	A		B		C
D			E	F	
G				H	
I		J		K	
		L			

2 Use these clues to complete the second cross-number puzzle on the PCM.

Clues across	Clues down
A 884 ÷ 4	**B** 201 × 8
C 12 × 8	**D** 79 × 8
E 8 × 8	**F** 92 × 8
F 90 × 8	**G** 52 × 8
G 168 ÷ 4	
H 488 ÷ 8	
I 66 × 4	

3 Work with a partner to make up your own cross-number puzzle clues for the third cross-number puzzle on the PCM.
   Try to make as many clues as you can that use what you know about multiplying and dividing by 4 and 8.

eXtra Swap puzzles with others and try to solve them.
Check your answers with each other.

Centres of enlargement

This picture has been enlarged twice. How can you measure how much it has been enlarged?

The small pentagon has lines from a point called the centre of enlargement to the corners, the most important points on the shape.

By extending the lines to double their lengths, new corner points are found and the enlarged figure is made.

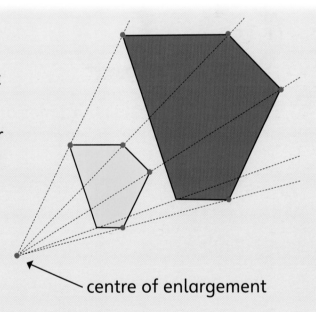

centre of enlargement

> Each side length has doubled, so the scale factor is ×2.

1 Use this method to enlarge the shape on PCM 44.

2 Draw your own shape on squared paper. Double its side lengths. Repeat with other shapes.

3 Explore drawing other shapes and enlarging them using different scale factors, including ×4.

 Explore following the lines backwards through the centre of enlargement. What do you notice?

Hands on a clock

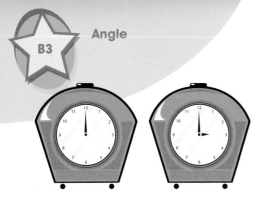

The hour hand of a clock makes one whole turn during 12 hours. From midday to 3 o'clock it turns through a quarter turn. A quarter turn is the same as a right angle, or 90 degrees, written 90°.

Write the angles in degrees turned by the hour hand.

1

2

3

4

5 Explore different pairs of times on a clock and the angle turned by the hour hand.

The minute hand makes a whole turn in one hour.
Write the angles in degrees turned by the minute hand.

6 15 minutes

7 30 minutes

8 45 minutes

9 10 minutes

10 35 minutes

11 55 minutes

What angle has the minute hand turned through?

12

13

eXtra

Predict which will be greater: the number of degrees the hour hand moves through in a week or the number of degrees the minute hand moves through in a day. Check your prediction.

Routes around shapes

Starting at the red point, this pentagon can be described as:

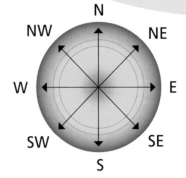

- 2 spaces north
- I space east
- I space south-east
- I space south-west
- I space west.

Shapes drawn on a 16-dot grid have inside angles that are multiples of $\frac{1}{2}$ a right angle. The inside angles of the pentagon are: I, I, I$\frac{1}{2}$, I, and I$\frac{1}{2}$ right angles.

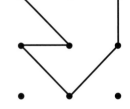

I Give compass directions to draw this shape. Start at the red point.

2 What are its inside angles? (Give them as numbers of right angles.)

3–5 Give compass directions to draw the shapes on PCM 45. Start at the **X**. Write the inside angles for each shape. Record the information in a table.

6 Explore other shapes that can be drawn on a 16-dot grid. Use square dotted paper. Record the features of the shapes in a table giving the numbers of sides, the compass directions and the inside angle sizes. Find their areas if you can.

Choose one of your shapes. Exchange the information you have recorded about your shape with another member of your group. Try to make each other's shapes. Compare the new shapes with the original shapes. Are they the same?

Mathematical worms

Prehistoric worms left tracks in areas of flat mud that are now fossilised. The tracks go straight, then suddenly turn in a clockwise direction. Mathematicians have designed special 'worm rules' to describe the tracks. The worms only move north, east, south or west, so square dot paper can be used to follow the rules and record the tracks.

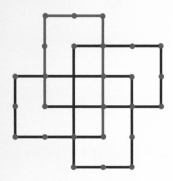

This track has the rule [3, 2, 4]. The red tracks show the worm moving north 3 steps, east 2 steps, then south 4 steps. It has used up its rule, so it starts again ... moving west 3, north 2, east 4, then south 3, and so on, until it repeats its tracks.

1–3 Work out the rules of the tracks on PCM 45.

4 Use dot paper and draw tracks using these rules:

[2, 3, 4]   [4, 2, 3]   [I, 2, 4]

[I, 3, 5]   [2, 4, 4]   [2, 2, 7]

Are there any patterns?

Compare the tracks. Which rules give the same tracks? Which tracks look similar, but are slightly different?

eXtra Explore other rules. What happens when a worm has a rule with four numbers? What about rules with five numbers? Find some general explanations for what happens.

British cities

PCM 46 shows an outline map of Britain.
The capital cities of England, Scotland, Wales and
Northern Ireland are marked.
The squares in the grid have sides of 100 km.

1   Label the columns of the grid with the letters A, B, C, …
    from west to east.
    Label the rows with the numbers 1, 2, 3, … from south to north.
    Each square now has a letter/number code, such as A1.

2   Find the codes for the squares where the capital cities are.
    Record them in the table on PCM 47.

3   Which cities are marked by dots on the map?
    Write their names on the map.
    Record the codes of their squares in the table.

4   Find out where the other cities listed in the table are on the map.
    Mark them on the map and write their names.
    Record the codes of their squares.

5   Which squares have more than one city in them?
    In each case, find the combined total population of the cities in these
    squares. You can use a calculator if you need to.

> How far do you think the four
> capital cities are from each other?

Choose any of the 100 km squares. Mark it out on a big
4 × 4 grid, where the sides of the squares represent 25 km.
Are there any cities already in your square? Find out
about other cities, towns, villages, or places of interest
located in your 16-square grid. Mark them in the correct
places in the grid and write their names.

Ant and elephant weights

A leafcutter ant weighs about 3 milligrams.
So 300 leafcutter ants weigh 1 gram.

A female adult elephant weighs about 3000 kilograms.

1000 micrograms = 1 milligram (mg)   1000 mg = 1 gram (g)
1000 g = 1 kilogram (kg)   1000 kg = 1 tonne

Copy this table.

Range	Animal	Range	Animal
1–9 mg	ants	100–999 g	
10–99 mg		1–9 kg	
100–999 mg		10–99 kg	
1–9 g		100–999 kg	
10–99 g		1–10 tonnes	elephants

Use reference books or the internet to answer these questions and complete the table.

1   What animals weigh about 10 times as much as an ant?

2   What animals weigh about 10 times as much as this? Keep finding animals that are 10 times as heavy, up to elephants.

3   Where would you put yourself in the table?

Continue your table and find animals or other things that are heavier than elephants. How heavy is the blue whale, the largest mammal on Earth? Then continue your table, finding things that are 10 times lighter. What things are 10 times lighter than ants?

Time facts

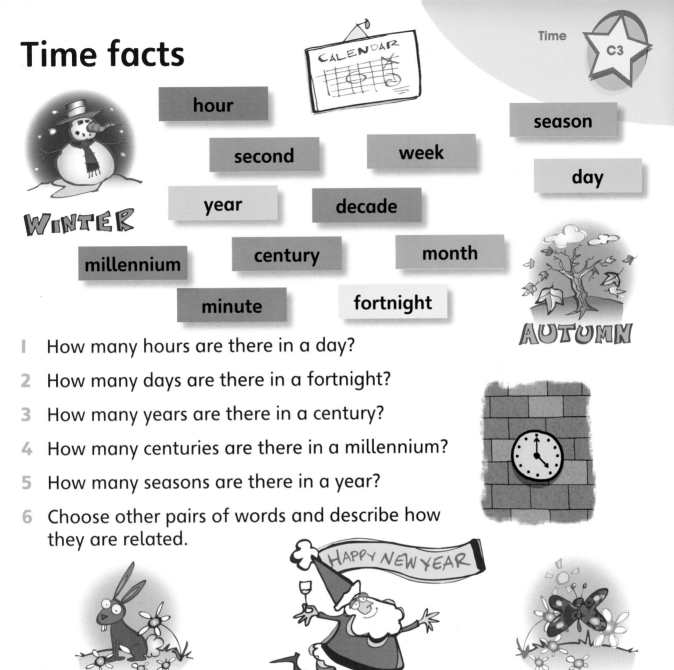

hour

season

second   week

day

year   decade

millennium   century   month

minute   fortnight

1 How many hours are there in a day?

2 How many days are there in a fortnight?

3 How many years are there in a century?

4 How many centuries are there in a millennium?

5 How many seasons are there in a year?

6 Choose other pairs of words and describe how they are related.

7 Arrange the 24 cards from PCM 50 in a complete chain, so that the question on each card is answered on the next.

- How many seconds are there in a day?
- How many days are there in a decade?
- How many weeks are there in a century?
- How many months are there in a millennium?

Use a calculator to help you if you need.

Calendars

Thirty days hath September,

April, June, and November;

All the rest have 31, except February clear,

Which has 28, or 29 in each leap year.

SEPTEMBER

S	M	T	W	T	F	S
					1	2
3	4	5	6	7	8	9
10	11	12	13	14	15	16
17	18	19	20	21	22	23
24	25	26	27	28	29	30

FEBRUARY

S	M	T	W			
3	4	5	6	7	8	9
10	11	12	13	14	15	16
17	18	19	20	21	22	23
24	25	26	27	28	29	30

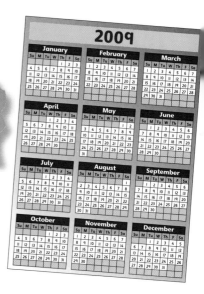

Look at this year's calendar.

1 Which day of the week occurs most often during the year?

2 Which months start on the same day and have the same number of days?

3 Which months start on a Sunday this year?   **What do you notice?**

4 What day will these months begin on next year?

Choose a month on a calendar and look at the numbers.

5 What are the patterns going down the columns?

6 If months were longer, how would the patterns continue?

7 Take a block of four numbers from the grid on a calendar.
   * Use a calculator to multiply the numbers diagonally.
   * What is the difference between your answers?
   * Repeat with other blocks of four numbers.

Is there a pattern?

3	4
10	11

ex**tra**   Investigate leap years. What is a leap year?
How do they work? How often do we have one?
What happens at the end of each century?
What happens at the end of each millennium?

Logic tracks

A logic track works by asking questions at the right points to sort things such as numbers or shapes. This is a logic track for numbers less than 20.

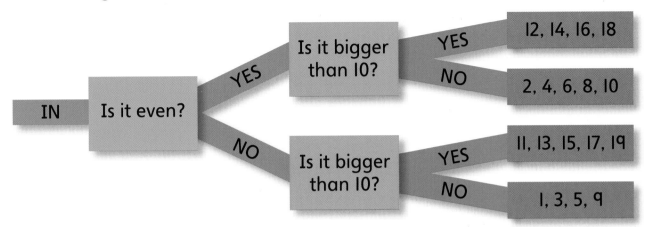

Example number properties
Is it an odd number?
Is it more than ...?
Is it a multiple of ...?
Do its digits add to ...?

Example shape properties
Is it symmetrical?
Does it have a right angle?
Are its diagonals equal?
Does it have parallel sides?

1 Write two questions about properties of numbers on blank cards. Write the second question twice. Place the cards on the blank logic track on PCM 51.

2 Put some 2-digit number cards through the track.

3 Swap the positions of the questions. What happens?

4 Repeat with other property questions and other numbers.

5 Now make up two questions about properties of shapes, and put different shapes through your logic track.
Try out your choices on the rest of your group.

 What are the links between logic tracks and Carroll diagrams and between logic tracks and Venn diagrams? Explore creating Carroll and Venn diagrams that will sort numbers or shapes in the same way as your logic track.

Three by three squares

In this 3 × 3 square, there is a different digit in each small square. The digits can be combined to make 2-digit numbers in both horizontal and vertical directions:

5	2	9
1	8	4
7	3	6

- 5 and 2 make 52
- 5 and 1 make 51.

1 Make the six horizontal 2-digit numbers and add them.

2 Make the six vertical 2-digit numbers and add them.

3 What is the difference between the two totals?

4 Add the two totals to find the score of this 3 × 3 square.

5 Use digit cards to make your own squares like this, and find their scores.

> Is there a pattern in where you place the digits?

6 Try to make a square with the biggest possible score.

 eXtra Shuffle digit cards 1–9. Pick a card at random. Put the card to one side, and replace it with a 0 card. You should now have eight numbers, plus a 0. Use these nine digits to make a 3 × 3 square. Work out the score. What is the largest possible score you can make with these nine digits?

Pentacircles and hexacircles

This is a **pentacircle**.
It is a large ring made of
five overlapping circles.

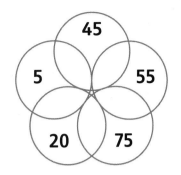

1 Copy this pentacircle onto PCM 52. Work out where to put numbers in the overlapping parts of the pentacircle so that the three numbers in each circle total 100. Use only multiples of 5, and do not use any number twice.

2 Use PCM 52 and make your own pentacircle totalling 100 in each circle. This time you can't use multiples of 5.

Five numbers in a pentacircle are only in one circle. They are the **outer circle** numbers. Their total is the **score** for that pentacircle.

3 What is the score of the pentacircle in question 1?

4 What is the total of the other five numbers (the inner circle) in the pentacircle in question 1?

5 What is the score of the pentacircle you made for question 2?

6 What is the total of the inner circle of numbers in your pentacircle?

7 Try to make a pentacircle with the largest possible score using PCM 52. The numbers in each circle must still add to 100.

8 Investigate similar rules for **hexacircles**, with six overlapping circles. You can only use multiples of 10, and each circle must add to 1000. Explore making these hexacircles using PCM 52.

Look at all the circles in the hexacircles making 1000 that your group has made. Explore the patterns of tens digits in the circles. What do these add up to? Can you explain why this is? Look at the hundreds digits. What do they add up to? Why?

Cryptarithm puzzles

In a cryptarithm puzzle, each letter stands for a digit from 0 to 9.

Use digit cards and try to solve each of these cryptarithm puzzles.

1 HES + THE = BEST ⟶ *Hint:* E = 2

2 I + DID = TOO

3 NO + NO + TOO = LATE

Is there more than one solution for any of them?

4 Try to solve this famous cryptarithm, made up by the mathematician Henry Dudeney:
SEND + MORE = MONEY

Hints: M must be I.
S + M must be at least 9, so S must be either 8 or 9.
The digits 3 and 4 are not used.

Henry Dudeney

It is hard to make cryptarithm puzzles where the words make sense and the digits add correctly. It's easier to make puzzles from correct calculations made with digit cards.
For example, 750 + 250 = 1000 can become ABC + DBC = ECCC.

5 Make up your own puzzles and swap with others in your group.

A 'doubly true' cryptarithm makes a correct calculation when it is solved and the words are also mathematically correct.
Try to solve these.

6 FORTY + TEN + TEN = SIXTY

7 THREE + THREE + TWO + TWO + ONE = ELEVEN

e**X**tra Make up your own cryptarithm puzzle that uses proper words. Try it on your group.

Finding differences

The numbers 400 and 500 both have a difference of 50 from 450.

Write the pairs of numbers that have these differences.

1 A difference of 100 from 325.

2 A difference of 250 from 400.

3 A difference of 125 from 350.

4 A difference of 215 from 530.

Use a set of six cards from PCM 53 (take all the cards with one letter on them – either A, B, C or D). Arrange the cards in a loop so that the question on each card is answered on the next card.

5 Record the six cards in a table. For example, the table below records these two cards:

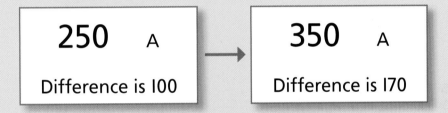

Number	Difference	Answer
250	100	350
350	170	180

6 Repeat for the other three sets of cards, and record the results. Use the cards to play a game with your group. One person puts down a card with 500 on. If the next player has a card that answers the question on the first card, they put it down. Continue playing until someone has no cards left. That person is the winner.

Arrange all 24 cards in one complete loop. There are four sets: A, B, C and D. You score 1 point every time you switch between these sets. Can you score at least 10 points?

Changing subtractions

Can you solve this subtraction?   234 – 185
What about this one?   100 – 51

You can change harder subtractions into easier ones, like this:
- Start with the hard subtraction: 234 – 185
- Subtract 100 from both numbers: 134 – 85
- Subtract 30 from both numbers: 104 – 55
- Subtract 4 from both numbers: 100 – 51 = 49

If you add/subtract the same amount to/from both numbers in a subtraction, the difference between the numbers stays the same.

Make these subtractions easier by subtracting equal amounts, then solve them.

| 1 156 – 38 | 2 172 – 46 | 3 140 – 89 |
| 4 525 – 244 | 5 647 – 169 | 6 323 – 186 |

> You don't always have to subtract hundreds, tens and units. Just subtract the digits that will help you.

Make these subtractions easier by adding equal amounts, then solve them.

| 7 135 – 65 | 8 87 – 43 | 9 245 – 213 |
| 10 396 – 175 | 11 248 – 169 | 12 561 – 326 |

> Which method do you prefer? Why?

13 Can you use number lines to show why the method of adding or subtracting equal amounts works?

eXtra
Make up some simple subtractions, such as 100 – 67 = 33. Use equal additions or subtractions to turn them into difficult-looking subtractions, such as 522 – 489. Try them out on a partner.

Multiplication arithmagons

In a multiplication arithmagon, the number in each square is the product of the numbers in the circles on either side.

> A product is the answer to a multiplication.

Copy these arithmagons onto PCM 55 and find the missing numbers.

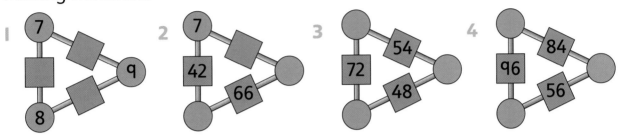

How many different solutions can you find if you are only given two numbers? Find out using these pairs of numbers.

5   36 and 54

6   25 and 60

7   49 and 91

8   Explore your own examples. Share ideas with your group.

How many solutions can you find if you only know one number in a square and the number in the circle opposite the square? Find out using these pairs of numbers (the number in the square is first).

9   24 and 9

10 72 and 5

11 90 and 7

12 Explore your own examples. Share ideas with your group.

13 Extend your investigations using the square, pentagonal and hexagonal arithmagons on PCM 55.

A triangular arithmagon has these numbers: 6, 7, 14, 42, 84, 98. Place all the numbers to make a correct arithmagon.
A second triangular arithmagon has two numbers hidden but these four numbers are showing: 15, 63, 105 and 135. Place them in an arithmagon and find the missing numbers.

Multiplying and dividing by 10, 100 and 1000

The linking cards on PCM 56 have both multiplication and division questions.

Warm up for playing the game by answering these questions.

1 8×10	2 3×60	3 6×100	4 4×200
5 3×1000	6 2×3000	7 0.5×10	8 3.6×10

9 These five cards belong to a set of six linking cards. Work out the answers to the questions, and the order the cards should go in. Find and record the missing card.

a	b	c	d	e
G **28** $30 \div 10$	G **500** $80 \div 4$	G **30** $280 \div 10$	G **3** 60×40	G **2400** 5×100

Take a set of six cards (labelled A, B, C or D). Place them in a complete chain, so that the question on each card is answered on the next card.

Repeat for the other three sets.

Play a game with your group, using all 24 cards. One person puts down a card with 70 on it. If the next person has a card with the answer to the first card, they put it down. If not, they miss a go. Continue until someone has no cards left. That person is the winner.

 e**X**tra

Design a new set of cards to run alongside sets A to D. Do not repeat any card used in the other sets. Use three multiplications and three divisions.

Repeated halving

These are some different ways of halving a square:

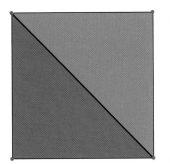 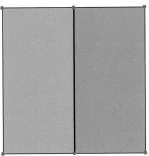  

Try out the first example of halving shown above.

1   After the first cutting line, what shape are the two halves?

2   How would you halve this shape?

3   Continue halving until you cannot halve any more.

> What do you notice about the new shapes?

4   Look at the pieces. What fractions of the original square are the smaller pieces?

5   If the smallest shape is worth Ip, how much are the other shapes worth?

6   How much is the original square worth?

Explore the fourth halving method shown above. Halve the square repeatedly using this method and record your findings.

 Using the shapes you saved from the first halving method, continue this spiral pattern. How far can you go?

Matching fractions, matching money

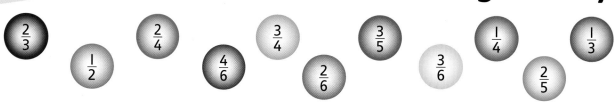

$\frac{2}{3}$ $\frac{1}{2}$ $\frac{2}{4}$ $\frac{4}{6}$ $\frac{3}{4}$ $\frac{2}{6}$ $\frac{3}{5}$ $\frac{3}{6}$ $\frac{1}{4}$ $\frac{2}{5}$ $\frac{1}{3}$

1   Which of these fractions is the same as a half?

2   Which fractions are more than a half?

3   Which fractions are less than a half?

4   Think of four fractions that are equal to a quarter.

5   Choose one of the fractions above. Think of four fractions that are equal to your chosen fraction.

6   Match the fraction cards from PCM 57 into eight equal pairs.

7   Record your results. For each pair, write a third equal fraction.

8   Use the money cards from PCM 57. Add pairs of amounts to make the targets in set A. Each pair includes one amount less than £1 and one amount more than £1.

Set A targets	£4·03	£3·99	£3·86	£3·85	£3·82
	£3·78	£3·67	£3·64	£3·55	£3·46

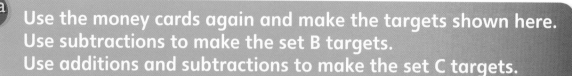

eXtra

Use the money cards again and make the targets shown here.
Use subtractions to make the set B targets.
Use additions and subtractions to make the set C targets.

Set B targets	£2·28	£2·25	£2·23	£2·15	£2·10
	£2·09	£2·17	£2·05	£2·02	£2·01

Set C targets	£3·95	£3·92	£3·85	£3·79	£3·57
	£3·52	£2·40	£2·26	£2·14	£2·07

Coins – old and new

Before 1971, we used a different system of currency in Britain.
Here are some of the coins used in the old system.

| half penny | penny | threepence | sixpence | shilling |

The old coins were worth the following amounts:

I **farthing**	= quarter of a penny
I **shilling**	= 12 pennies
I **florin**	= 24 pennies = 2 shillings
I **crown**	= 60 pennies = quarter of a pound
I **pound**	= 240 pennies = 20 shillings

Find the totals of the following amounts in pennies.

I 2 crowns, I shilling and sixpence

2 I pound, 3 florins and 8 half pennies

3 6 shillings, 4 threepences and I farthing

How much change would you get from I pound if you paid these
amounts? Give the change in pennies.

4 2 crowns and 2 florins

5 3 crowns and 3 shillings

6 8 florins, 2 shillings and 4 farthings

eXtra

In the old system, I pound was worth 240 old pennies.
Now, I pound is worth 100 new pennies. There were 20
shillings in I pound, so I shilling in new money would be 5p.
Can you convert any of the other old coins to new money?